Future Energy

Fossil Fuels

Julie Richards

A+

This edition first published in 2004 in the United States of America by
Smart Apple Media.

Smart Apple Media
1980 Lookout Drive
North Mankato
Minnesota 56003

Library of Congress Cataloging-in-Publication Data

Richards, Julie.
   Fossil fuels / by Julie Richards.
   p. cm. — (Future energy)

   Contents: What is energy?—Fossil fuels as a source of energy—Where do fossil
   fuels come from?—Fossil fuels through history—Early fossil-fuel technology—
   Modern fossil-fuel technology—Finding fossil fuels—Processing fossil fuels—Fossil
   fuels at work—Fossil fuels and the environment—Fossil fuels in the future—
   Advantages and disadvantages of fossil fuels.

   ISBN 1-58340-334-5
   1. Fossil fuels—Juvenile literature. [1. Fossil fuels.] I. Title.
   TP318.3.R53 2003
   333.793'2—dc21   2002044640

First Edition
9 8 7 6 5 4 3 2 1

First published in 2003 by
MACMILLAN EDUCATION AUSTRALIA PTY LTD
627 Chapel Street, South Yarra, Australia 3141

Associated companies and representatives throughout the world.

Edited by Anna Fern
Text and cover design by Cristina Neri, Canary Graphic Design
Illustrations by Nives Porcellato and Andy Craig
Photo research by Legend Images

Printed in Thailand

Acknowledgements
The author and the publisher are grateful to the following for permission to
reproduce copyright material:

Cover photograph: oil rig, courtesy of Digital Vision.

Australian Picture Library/Corbis, p. 15; Corbis Digital Stock, pp. 13, 16 (left),
17, 18, 24, 30; DaimlerChrysler AG, pp. 26, 27, 29; Digital Vision, pp. 1, 25;
Getty Images, pp. 5 (bottom), 6 (top), 8 (top), 9 (top), 10, 14, 21 (top—all), 23;
Kvaerner Pulping Oy, p. 28; Wade Hughes/Lochman Transparencies, p. 21
(bottom); Mary Evans Picture Library, p. 11; Photolibrary.com, pp. 4, 12, 22;
Reuters, pp. 8 (bottom), 9 (bottom).

Contents

Glossary words
When a word is printed in **bold** you can look up its meaning in the glossary on page 31.

What is energy?

Energy makes the world work. People, plants, and animals need energy to live and grow. Most of the world's machines are powered by energy that comes from burning coal, oil, and gas. Coal, oil, and natural gas are known as fossil fuels. Burning fossil fuels makes the air dirty. This is harmful to people and damages the environment.

Scientists are not sure how much longer fossil fuels will last. It depends on whether or not new sources of this type of energy are found and how carefully we use what is left. Scientists do know that if we keep using fossil fuels as fast as we are now, they *will* run out. An energy source that can be used up is called non-renewable. A renewable source is one that never runs out. The world cannot rely on fossil fuels as a source of energy for everything. We need to find other sources of safe, clean, renewable energy to power the machines we have come to depend on.

These are the fossilized remains of a fish. Fossil fuels are the plants and animals that died millions of years ago and turned into coal, oil, and gas.

Fossil
Fuels

Fossil fuels as a source of energy

All living things need energy to grow and stay healthy. Animals and people get their energy from food. The plants that people and animals eat get their energy from the Sun.

Fossil fuels are made from what is left of the plants and animals that lived millions of years ago. After they died, they became buried beneath layers of rock and soil. Some of them turned into coal. Others turned into oil and natural gas. Burning fossil fuels releases the energy inside the coal, oil, or gas. This energy is used to power transportation and to make the electricity needed to power the world's machines. When fossil fuels are burned, they release the energy of the Sun that was captured more than 300 million years ago.

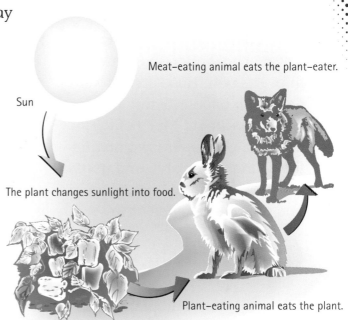

Sun

Meat-eating animal eats the plant-eater.

The plant changes sunlight into food.

Plant-eating animal eats the plant.

Plants store energy from the Sun. The Sun's energy is passed along the food chain, giving energy to living things.

The energy in coal is changed into heat when it burns.

Where do fossil fuels come from?

Fossil fuels are formed deep inside the Earth. About 300 million years ago, the Earth was much warmer and wetter than it is now. Huge oceans were filled with billions of tiny plants and sea animals. Much of the land was covered by swamp and thick jungle. Coal, oil, and natural gas are made from these plants and animals in different ways.

Coal

When the trees and plants died, they sank into the soft mud of the swamps, and began to **decay**. More trees and plants fell on top of them, pressing them deeper into the mud and turning them into a brown, spongy mixture called peat. The peat was pressed so hard that all the water was squeezed out of it. When the peat became harder, heavier, and darker, it had turned into brown coal. The brown coal was pressed even harder and deeper, until it became black coal.

Long ago, plants captured the Sun's energy. When the plants died, the Sun's energy was trapped inside them.

Over millions of years, dead trees and plants turned into peat and coal.

1 Living trees and plants

2 When they died, these trees and plants sank into the swamp and were covered in mud. Over millions of years, they turned into peat.

3 As layers of trees and plants built up, their weight pressed down harder and harder until the peat changed into brown coal and black coal.

Black coal seams

Fossil Fuels

Oil and natural gas

The plants and animals that lived in the oceans sank to the bottom when they died. Their bodies were covered by sand and bits of rock carried into the ocean by rivers. The plants and animals were pressed into the **sea-bed** in the same way as the plants on the land. Beneath the sea, they turned into a thick, black liquid called oil. The gas given off by their decaying bodies became trapped underground, too. This gas is called natural gas.

It has taken nature millions of years to make fossil fuels. Once they are burned to release their energy, they cannot be used again. Something that can only be used once is called non-renewable. The world is using fossil fuels more quickly than nature can make them.

Over millions of years, the sea plants and animals turned into oil and gas.

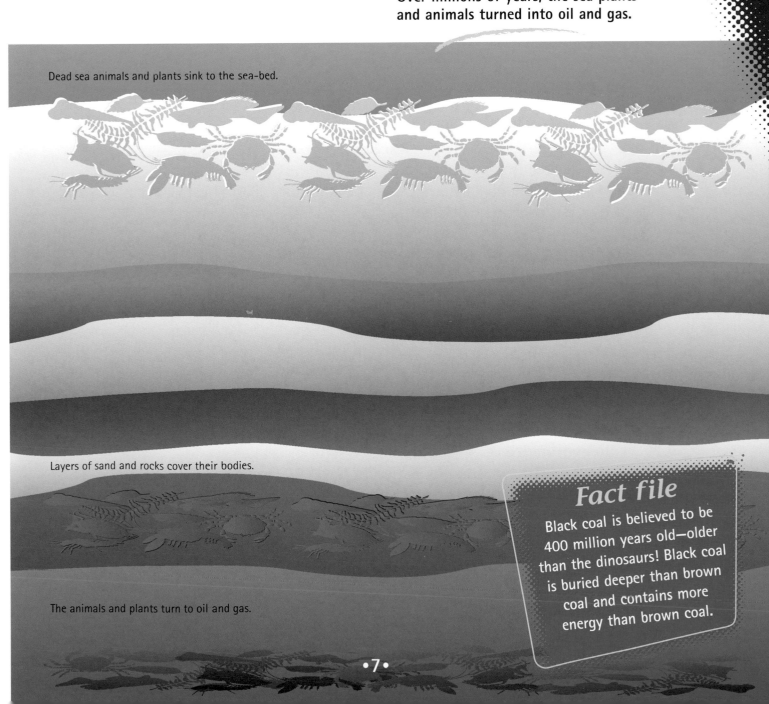

Dead sea animals and plants sink to the sea-bed.

Layers of sand and rocks cover their bodies.

The animals and plants turn to oil and gas.

Fact file

Black coal is believed to be 400 million years old—older than the dinosaurs! Black coal is buried deeper than brown coal and contains more energy than brown coal.

Fossil fuels through history

People have known about coal, oil, and natural gas for thousands of years.

Ancient use of fossil fuels

Coal

Many ancient peoples discovered that coal gave off heat when it burned. They used it for warmth, to cook their food, and to frighten away dangerous animals. Three thousand years ago, the Chinese began burning coal instead of wood. Coal burned much hotter, and this allowed them to melt soft metals such as copper. **Archeologists** (say *ar-kee-olo-jists*) in different parts of the world have found ancient tools embedded in layers of coal. This tells us that many ancient peoples used coal.

This bowl was baked using the heat from burning coal. Heating makes clay stronger and waterproof.

Oil and natural gas

Oil that oozed from cracks in the ground was heated by the Sun and turned into a thick, gluey substance called pitch. Pitch was painted onto boats and shelters to waterproof them. Bunches of sticks dipped in pitch and then set alight became bright-burning torches. As long ago as 900 B.C., the Chinese found oil and natural gas in the saltwater **wells** they dug. The gas was burned to **evaporate** the water, leaving the salt behind. The oil and gas were sent through bamboo pipes for heating and cooking.

The dead bodies of important ancient Egyptians were sometimes painted with oil to stop them from decaying too quickly.

Fossil Fuels

Modern use of fossil fuels

Coal

Muscle power was the first source of energy for doing work. When people invented machines, a reliable source of energy was needed to keep them running. One of the world's most important inventions was the steam-powered engine. Steam was made by burning coal to heat boilers filled with water inside the steam engine. Soon, many machines were running on steam. Huge steam **locomotives** and steamships carried people and goods across great distances.

Steam was found to be more reliable than using wind-powered boats or horse-drawn carts for transportation. Wind-powered boats could be stuck at sea for many weeks if the wind did not blow. Horses needed food, water, and rest during the journey. The roads they traveled were rough and filled with holes, and many horses fell and injured themselves. Others would run away when they were frightened by strange noises or wild animals.

Oil and natural gas

In the 1850s, people digging for salt in the United States discovered oily rocks. The oil was collected and used in some medicines and as fuel in lamps. Until this time, most of the oil used by modern people was made by melting the fat from whales and other animals. Natural gas was often found in the same places as water and oil. Natural gas is invisible and has no smell. People thought it too dangerous to be useful and nobody knew how to collect and store it.

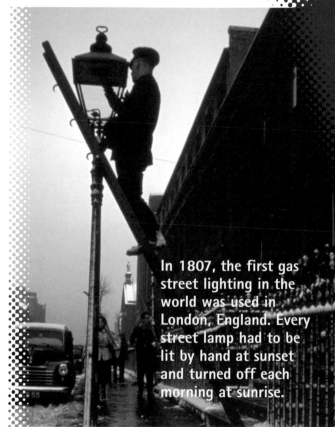

In 1807, the first gas street lighting in the world was used in London, England. Every street lamp had to be lit by hand at sunset and turned off each morning at sunrise.

The steam locomotive was one of the world's most important inventions. It allowed people to travel long distances more quickly and comfortably.

Fact file

In 1792, an English inventor named William Murdock heated coal inside an airtight glass. The coal gave off a gas. Murdock began making his own coal gas, which he used to light his home.

Early fossil-fuel technology

At first, fossil fuels were easy to find. Lumps of coal lay on the surface of the land and oil oozed from cracks in the ground. Natural gas escaped from these cracks, too. Gas could be seen when lightning struck and the gas caught fire. When these sources were used up, people had to dig underground to find new ones.

Coal

The first coalmines were extremely dangerous places. They often flooded with water or filled with poisonous gases. The roofs caved in and many miners were killed and injured. Before machines were invented, the miners used only **picks** and shovels.

Oil and natural gas

The world's first **commercial** oil well was drilled on August 27, 1859, in Pennsylvania, by Edwin Drake. The drill was powered by a steam engine. The well was 69 feet (21 m) deep and produced 422 gallons (1,600 l) of oil every day. In 1885, Robert Bunsen invented a burner that mixed air with natural gas. The Bunsen burner showed how gas could be used to provide heat for cooking and warmth for buildings. As soon as people realized that oil and gas had many uses, they began to drill for them wherever they thought they might be found.

Fact file

In the 1800s, small horses called pit ponies were taken down the mines to pull carts loaded with coal. Many pit ponies never saw daylight until they were too old or sick to work any more.

Without machines, mining was slow and exhausting. The lamps used to light the miners's way often caused gases inside the mine to explode.

Fossil Fuels

Modern fossil-fuel technology

During the 1800s, there were two big changes to the way people lived —electricity and the automobile. Inventors studying electricity soon realized it would be the best source of energy for all the new machines. The more uses they found for electricity, the more machines they invented.

Inventors of the first automobiles heated oil to produce **gasoline**. Gasoline was a better source of energy because only a small tank was needed to carry it. Steam-powered vehicles had to be large enough to carry the heavy loads of coal and water needed for their boilers wherever they went. Most steam-powered vehicles needed a driver and someone to keep the fire going beneath the boilers. Only one person was needed to drive an automobile.

Machines and automobiles have made the world rely so much on fossil fuels that they are beginning to run out. The dangerous gases released when fossil fuels are burned can be seen as a layer of dirty brown air above the world's busy cities. These gases contain chemicals that change into **acid** when it rains. If we are to keep using fossil fuels, we need to find ways to make them last longer and to make them cleaner to use.

In 1879, when Thomas Edison invented the electric lightbulb, everybody wanted one. Edison had to invent a way to carry electricity into people's homes. In 1882, he opened the world's first power station in New York. Electricity was carried through cables to 52 customers in nearby buildings.

Mining and drilling

Once coal, oil, and natural gas have been found, they must be brought out from under the ground. Coal is mined. Oil and natural gas are drilled. Mining coal and drilling for oil and gas is very hard work. It can also be very dangerous. Finding fossil fuels and bringing them out of the ground is getting more difficult. These sources of energy are becoming scarce because they cannot be renewed.

Coalmining

Coal is mined in different ways, depending on how close to the surface the coal seam is.

Strip mining

If a thin layer of soil and rock covers the coal, it is easy to reach. The rock containing the coal is shattered by explosives and scooped up by huge earth-moving machines. A coalmine like this is called a strip, open-cut, or open-cast mine. Strip mining is used a lot in the U.S. and Australia. It is the cheapest kind of mining, but it leaves enormous, ugly scars on the land.

Strip mines leave huge, ugly scars on the land.

Fossil
Fuels

Powerful machines like these cutting drills do nearly all the work in modern mines.

Underground mining

When the coal is deep underground, the miners have to dig down to reach it. The holes they dig are called shafts. Some shafts are deeper than 1,900 feet (600 m), but most are about 300 feet (90 m) deep.

A deep mine is like an underground town. There are offices and workshops and special vehicles to take the miners to where they will be working. The miners travel up and down the shafts in elevators. The shafts also let fresh air into the mine.

Fact file

There are different types of underground coalmining. Some coal is mined by letting the roof collapse behind the cutting machine as it moves through one of the mine tunnels. This is called longwall mining. The cutting machine is taken apart underground and moved to another tunnel where it is needed. It takes two weeks to take the machine apart, because it is so large. Another type is called room–and–pillar mining. As the cutting machine moves through, pillars of coal are left to support the roof.

The miners dig tunnels outward from the bottom of the shaft. They use giant cutting machines with sharp teeth. As the teeth spin, they bite into the coal and scrape chunks of it out of the seam.

The coal is loaded into wagons or placed on a **conveyor belt** and carried to the bottom of the shaft, where it is tipped into **skips**. The skips are lifted to the surface. Large chunks of coal are crushed into smaller pieces to make them easier to clean and transport. The coal is fed into a water-filled tank. The clean coal floats to the surface.

Drilling for oil and natural gas on land

Oil and natural gas are brought to the surface using a sharp-toothed drill attached to a pipe. As the drill spins, it cuts a hole through the rock. As the drill goes deeper, extra pieces of pipe are added behind it. Bending the pipe allows the drill to be steered through the rock in any direction. Special mud is pumped down inside the pipe to cool the drill and stop pieces of rock from jamming the drill teeth.

Oil is trapped underground at high pressure. The air inside a blown-up balloon is under tremendous pressure, too. If you stick a pin in the balloon, the air rushes out. When the drill breaks through the rock and the pressure is released, the oil can spurt out from the pipe high into the air. Modern oil wells have taps that control the flow of the oil.

To release gas trapped inside rock, water is pumped at high pressure into the rock until it cracks. A substance like sand, or tiny glass beads, is added to the water. This substance stays behind in the cracks, keeping them open after the water drains away.

Drilling for oil and gas on land

How steam is injected into an oil well to increase pressure

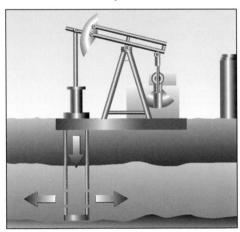

Nodding donkey pushes steam into oil well.

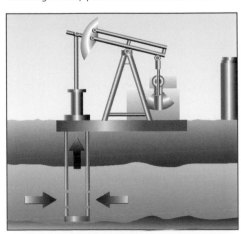

Oil is forced up into pipe. Thick, heavy oil is heated by steam to make it thinner so that it flows faster.

Drilling at sea

A lot of oil and gas is found beneath the sea-bed. To reach it, drilling platforms are anchored to the sea-bed on huge legs. The oil is stored in tanks and pumped on board ships called tankers. Tankers carry the oil and gas to **refineries** on land. Oil and gas can also be sent through a pipe that runs along the sea-bed.

Not all platforms are fixed to the sea-bed. Some are floating. Drill ships have a tall **derrick** on top of their deck. In very deep water, an anchor cannot be used to keep the ship in one place. Drill ships use special propellers called thrusters to keep the ship steady while they drill. In very shallow water, the derrick and buildings can sit on an **artificial** island built of sand.

Platform perils

Most oil platforms in the North Sea are 755 feet (230 m) high and weigh 38,580 tons (35,000 t). Most of the weight is perched on top of the legs. The North Sea is very stormy. The waves can be as high as 100 feet (30 m), with winds blowing at 75 miles (120 km) per hour. Sometimes, oil platforms can come loose from the sea-bed.

Oil platforms can drill up to 16,000 feet (5,000 m) beneath the sea. If the sea was drained away, the platform would be as tall as a skyscraper.

Helipad for helicopters to carry workers to and from the platform.

A derrick holds the drilling equipment.

The workers live on the platform for months at a time.

Legs fix the platform to the sea-bed.

Processing fossil fuels

Fossil fuels have to be transported to wherever they are needed or to the places that change them into products we can use.

Coal

Trains, trucks, or **barges** are used to transport coal. Sometimes, the coal is mixed with water or oil and sent down a pipe instead. Most of the coal is sent to power stations to be burned to make electricity.

Oil and gas

The easiest way to move oil and gas about on land is to pump them through a pipeline. In colder parts of the world, the pipeline has to be **insulated** to keep the oil warm, or it will stop moving. If the oil and gas platforms are a long way out at sea, tankers carry the oil and gas to land. Some of the tankers are so long, the crew use bicycles to get from one end of the tanker to the other. Gas has to be cooled so that it changes into a liquid and takes up less space. It is stored in **spherical** containers inside the ship. Road tankers are used to carry gasoline and gas from refineries to service stations.

An oil pipeline

Fact file

The world's longest oil pipeline stretches 2,350 miles (3,787 km) across Canada. The longest gas pipeline is also in Canada. It is 8,690 miles (14,000 km) long.

Fossil
Fuels

The oil refinery

The oil that comes out of the ground is called crude oil. Crude oil is dirty and contains dangerous gases. An oil refinery is where crude oil is cleaned and made into products such as gasoline.

Separating the oil

Oil is separated into different materials by heating it inside a special tower. Gases rise to the top of the tower, while thick oil, wax, and tar stay near the bottom. Sometimes, chemicals are added to the oil to change it into other substances. Pipes leave the tower at different heights carrying the new substances that have been separated or made from the oil.

Natural gas

Natural gas is often found in the same places as oil and is brought to the surface at the same time. The gas is separated from the oil and taken to a treatment plant. Natural gas is a mixture of different chemicals. Some of them are poisonous and need to be removed. After the gas has been separated and cleaned, a smell is added to it. This smell makes it easy to detect a gas leak.

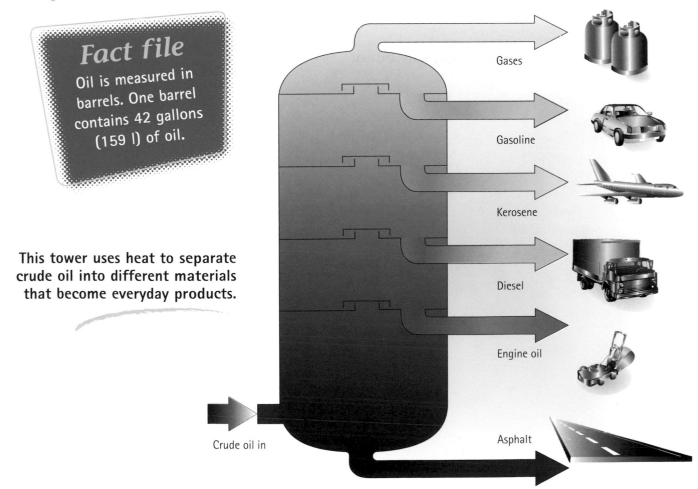

Fact file

Oil is measured in barrels. One barrel contains 42 gallons (159 l) of oil.

This tower uses heat to separate crude oil into different materials that become everyday products.

Gases

Gasoline

Kerosene

Diesel

Engine oil

Crude oil in

Asphalt

Fossil fuels at work

Fossil fuels have many uses. Most of the world's energy comes from burning fossil fuels because they are fairly easy and cheap to find. Powering transportation and making electricity are the two main uses for fossil fuels.

Coal

Power stations

All around the world, coal is used to make electricity. Inside a power station, coal is crushed into a dust and blown into a giant oven called a furnace. When the coaldust burns, it releases energy in the form of heat. This heat is used to boil water. The steam from the boiling water spins a giant wheel called a turbine. A **generator** changes this spinning movement into electricity. Powerlines carry the electricity to buildings. Electricity is used for heating, lighting, and cooking. It also powers machines in factories and equipment in hospitals, offices, and schools.

Power stations are not very **efficient**. Nearly two-thirds of the energy contained inside the fuel they burn is wasted because a lot of heat escapes. Power stations also pollute the air with harmful gases and bits of **soot**.

Steel

Steel is made by heating coal and rocks that contain iron inside a furnace until they melt together. The **molten** metal is shaped into many useful things, such as railroad tracks, car parts, and girders used for building. Coal is also used to make things such as waterproofing chemicals, insect spray, and mothballs.

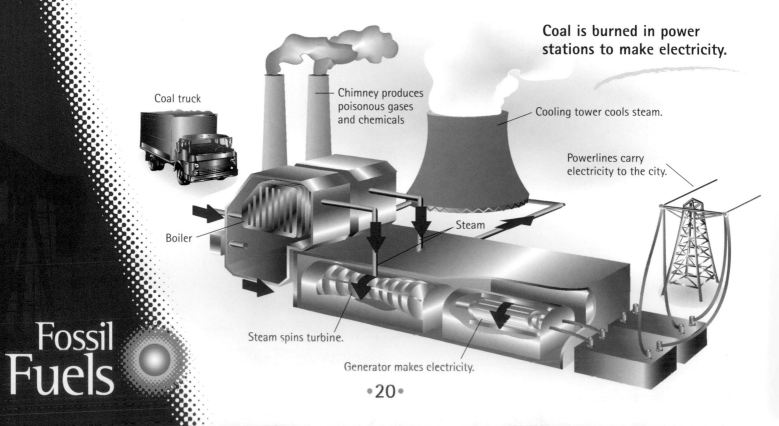

Coal is burned in power stations to make electricity.

Coal truck

Chimney produces poisonous gases and chemicals

Cooling tower cools steam.

Powerlines carry electricity to the city.

Boiler

Steam

Steam spins turbine.

Generator makes electricity.

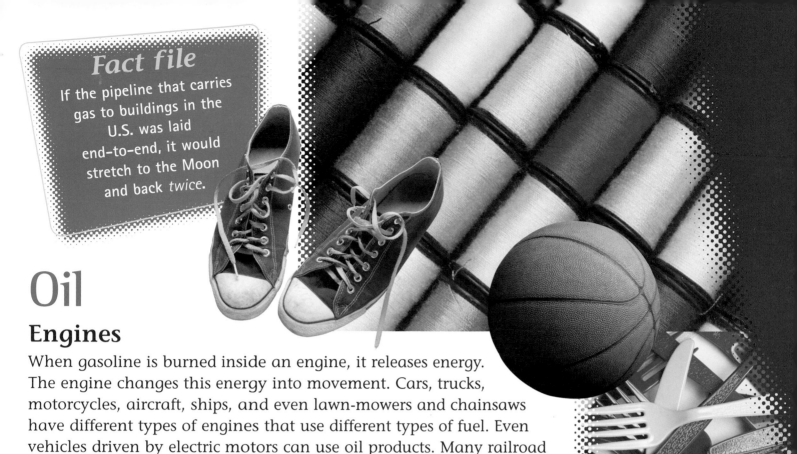

Oil

Engines

When gasoline is burned inside an engine, it releases energy. The engine changes this energy into movement. Cars, trucks, motorcycles, aircraft, ships, and even lawn-mowers and chainsaws have different types of engines that use different types of fuel. Even vehicles driven by electric motors can use oil products. Many railroad locomotives and submarines use diesel engines to drive the electricity generators that power their electric motors. Harmful, smelly gases and dangerous chemicals escape into the air as the fuel is burned.

Gas

Natural gas that has been treated at a gas plant is piped to buildings for heating and cooking. Gas is a very useful fuel because it is **portable**. A lot of gas can be squeezed into a small space inside a tank. This cannot be done with coal or oil. Campers, mountaineers, and explorers can take bottled gas anywhere with them to run stoves and heaters. A hot-air balloon carries bottles of gas to heat the air inside the balloon and make it rise. Other gases made from crude oil are used in **aerosol** cans to push the spray out.

When the air inside a hot-air balloon is heated by burning gas, it makes the air become lighter, lifting the balloon from the ground.

Many chemicals are produced from crude oil in a refinery. These chemicals are used to make many everyday things. The most important product to come out of an oil refinery is the fuel needed to power the world's transportation engines.

•21•

Fossil fuels and the environment

Everyone uses fossil fuels each day by burning gasoline in cars or using electricity. When fossil fuels are burned, they release energy. They also release gases, chemicals, and tiny pieces of soot that are harmful to people and the environment.

Pollution or smog can hang over a city for days if there is no wind to blow it away.

Air pollution and acid rain

A blanket of dirty air hangs over most of the world's cities. This air becomes trapped if there is no wind to blow it away. People suffer from lung diseases because there is no way to remove the dirty air. Acid rain forms when some chemicals mix with water in the air. Acid rain is slowly poisoning rivers, lakes, and forests. Even stone statues that have stood for thousands of years are being eaten away quickly by acid rain.

Greenhouse effect

Carbon dioxide is a harmful gas that is produced when fossil fuels are burned. Carbon dioxide traps the Sun's heat in the Earth's atmosphere. So much carbon dioxide is being produced and trapping so much heat in the atmosphere, that the Earth is becoming warmer. This is called the greenhouse effect. Scientists believe the greenhouse effect is changing the world's weather. It could also melt too much ice at the North and South poles, making the sea level rise. Some low-lying countries might disappear under water.

Fact file

Planting more trees can help keep the air clean. Trees remove carbon dioxide from the air and release oxygen back into it. Over their lifetime, some trees can soak up as much carbon dioxide as a car can produce in a year.

Fossil Fuels

Oil spills

Burning is not the only way fossil fuels harm the environment. Tankers can leak oil into the sea. The oil floats on top of the water, sticking to the feathers of birds and the fur of seals. Animals coated in oil are unable to fly or swim. They are easily attacked by **predators** or starve because they cannot catch their food. Creatures that eat the oil-covered animals are poisoned. The oil washes up onto beaches in a thick, horrible sludge.

Cleaning up after an oil spill

Harsh chemical detergents and blasts of high-speed water are used to clean up oil spills on rocks and beaches. Machines can skim oil from the surface of the water and store it in tanks. Special floats are also used as a fence to stop the oil from spreading out from the tanker. Smaller tankers try to pump as much of the oil left in the tanker into their own cargo space to reduce the amount left to spill. It is very expensive to clean up an oil spill. Many of the cleaning chemicals are just as harmful to the environment and the wildlife as the oil.

Fact file

The worst oil spill in the world happened on March 24, 1989, when the oil tanker *Exxon Valdez* crashed into a rocky reef near Alaska. Eleven million gallons (41 million l) of oil gushed from the tanker—enough to fill 125 Olympic swimming pools. The oil was washed up onto 1,300 miles (2,080 km) of beaches. It killed 250,000 seabirds, 2,800 otters, 300 seals, 250 eagles, 22 killer whales, and an unknown number of fish. Years later, the environment is still recovering.

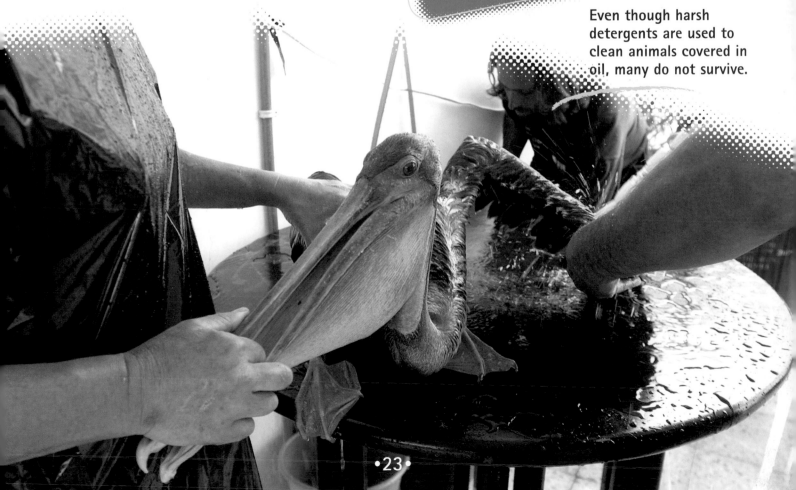

Even though harsh detergents are used to clean animals covered in oil, many do not survive.

Fossil fuels in the future

Fossil fuels are non-renewable energy sources that are running out. We are using them much faster than nature can make them. Every day, across the world, more than 100,000 new cars appear on the roads.

Each year, the world needs more fossil fuels to power its machines than it did before. And every year, the problems caused by burning fossil fuels become worse.

What is left in the ground?

Geologists are looking for new sources of fossil fuels. There is still coal, oil, and gas left in the ground, but the fossil fuels that are easily reached are beginning to run low. Mining and drilling what is left will be more difficult, expensive, and dangerous.

Some power stations have underground pipes that carry escaping heat to nearby buildings. This saves energy from being wasted.

Fact file
It takes 10 feet (3 m) of dead plant material to make 1 foot (30 cm) of coal.

Fossil Fuels

Drilling deep under the ocean for methane is a very dangerous job.

Getting more oil out of the ground

Some scientists believe that fast-growing **microbes** can help bring leftover oil to the surface. The gas produced as the microbes fed would collect in the oil reservoirs. The pressure of the gas would rapidly increase and push the oil upwards. Some oil is always washed away when water is pumped into a reservoir to create pressure. If the water carried billions of microbes and their food, the microbes could multiply enough to block off the cracks the oil washed into.

Other scientists are working on new chemicals that will stop oil droplets clinging to rock. Carbon dioxide gas has also been pumped into oil wells. Carbon dioxide is a poisonous gas produced by power stations as they burn fossil fuels. Instead of allowing this gas to escape into the air, it might be possible to capture it and use it to push leftover oil towards the surface.

Methane—a new fossil fuel source?

Methane is a natural gas that burns more cleanly and efficiently than any other fossil fuel. Geologists are working out how to drill vast amounts of frozen methane gas found beneath the ocean floor. The gas will need to be melted at the bottom of the well by a heater. It would then be piped aboard a drilling ship and cooled into a liquid for storage.

The methane might provide as much as 80,000 times more energy than is left in other fossil fuels. Drilling this deep-ocean methane is a very dangerous job. When it is disturbed, the gas swells to 160 times its size and bubbles explosively to the surface. It could easily sink a drill ship or destroy a drilling platform.

Making fossil fuels last

If no new sources of fossil fuels are found, we will have to use what is left very carefully. New technologies are being developed to make our use of fossil-fuel energy more efficient than it is now.

Micro-turbines

In the future, people may generate all the electricity they need in their own homes using a micro-turbine. Micro-turbines work in much the same way as the larger turbines in power stations do. The micro-turbines could run on a much cleaner and energy-efficient gas such as methane. The gas would be safely stored at home, making the energy supply cheaper and more reliable.

Hybrid cars

A hybrid car is a car that can switch between different energy sources. Some hybrid cars can use both gasoline and other liquid fuels. Others can use either gasoline or electricity. Hybrid electric cars have two motors to handle the two different fuel sources and drive the generator that charges the **batteries**. A hybrid car built in Australia was successfully tested in 2001. It used half the amount of gasoline a normal car would use and released fewer gases into the air. The heavy batteries carried by electric cars could soon be replaced by fuel cells.

This hybrid car can use either gasoline or electricity to power its engine. It produces less pollution and uses less gasoline than a normal car.

Fossil
Fuels

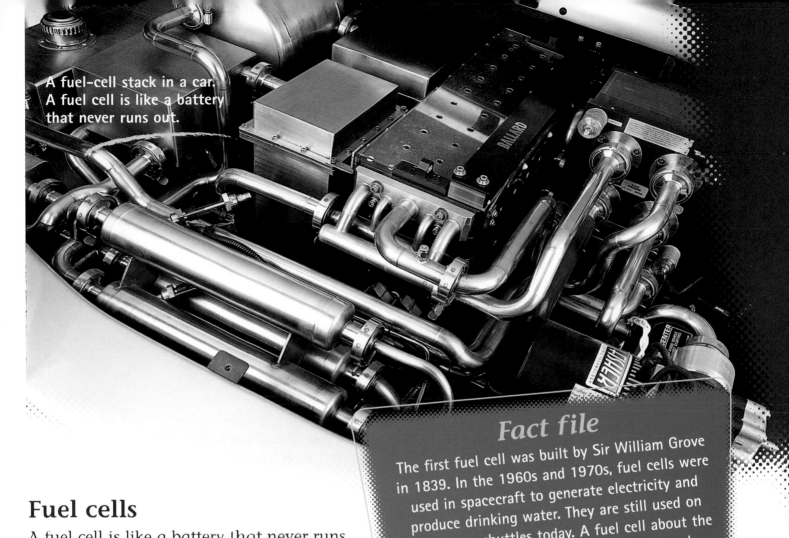

A fuel-cell stack in a car. A fuel cell is like a battery that never runs out.

Fuel cells

A fuel cell is like a battery that never runs out. Fuel cells and batteries both use a chemical reaction to produce energy, however, a battery runs out because its fuel supply is limited to what is stored inside it. A fuel cell does not run out because the fuel and air making the energy inside it are fed into the fuel cell continuously. Fuel cells can be made to use many different types of non-polluting, renewable fuels, including methane gas, hydrogen, and alcohol-based fuels. Fuel cells can be stacked together when more power is needed, and are especially useful in **remote** areas, where there is no proper electricity supply. Fuel cells create much less pollution than fossil fuels.

Fact file

The first fuel cell was built by Sir William Grove in 1839. In the 1960s and 1970s, fuel cells were used in spacecraft to generate electricity and produce drinking water. They are still used on board space shuttles today. A fuel cell about the size of a refrigerator could provide enough electricity for 500 houses. Two thousand would produce the same amount of electricity as a large coal-fired power station. A fuel cell is more energy-efficient than most coal-fired power stations.

Fuel cells can be powered by hydrogen gas. The only waste produced when hydrogen is used to make electricity is water, so fuel cells are a very clean source of energy. There is plenty of hydrogen available because water is made from hydrogen. The hydrogen is separated from the water using electricity. If the electricity used to do this comes from a renewable energy source such as the Sun or the wind, then hydrogen is truly a source of clean, renewable energy.

Cleaner use of fossil fuels

There are ways to make fossil fuels cleaner and safer for people and the environment.

Clean coal technology

Although coal is washed before it is burned in a power station, some of the poisonous chemicals it contains cannot be washed away. They are only released when the coal is burned. Trying to remove these chemicals before burning is very expensive. Instead, modern power stations have scrubbers. A scrubber is a mixture of water and crushed rock called limestone. A scrubber is sprayed into the smoke rising from the boiler as the coal burns. It soaks up the chemicals like a sponge so they are not carried up the chimney and into the atmosphere.

Turning coal into a gas

When coal is heated and blasted with steam, it changes into a gas. Changing coal into gas gets rid of nearly all the poisonous chemicals. When the gas is burned, it creates new gases which are hot enough to boil water to steam. The steam spins a turbine and electricity is generated. Some of the new gases are changed into liquids and used to make plastic and a type of liquid fuel that can be burned in car engines instead of gasoline.

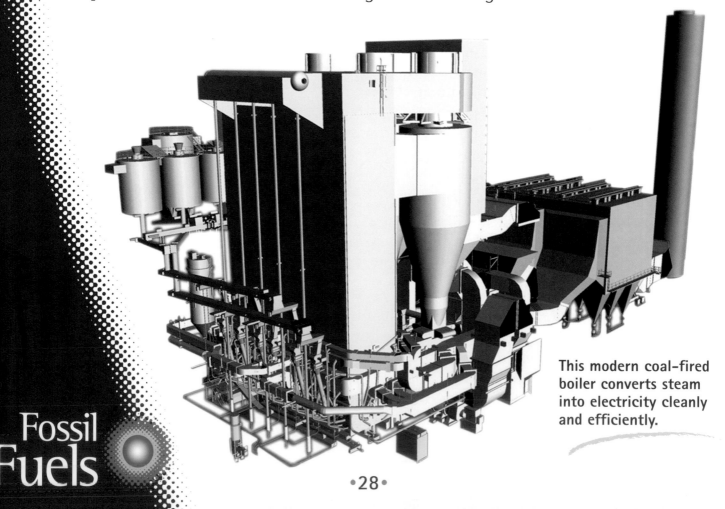

This modern coal-fired boiler converts steam into electricity cleanly and efficiently.

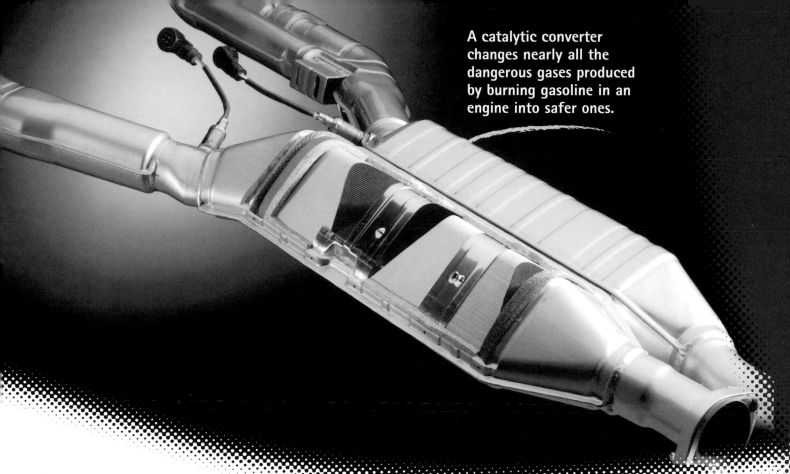

A catalytic converter changes nearly all the dangerous gases produced by burning gasoline in an engine into safer ones.

Cleaner transportation

Oil refineries used to add lead to gasoline to make it burn more efficiently inside an engine. Lead is a very poisonous metal. If there is lots of lead in the air, people breathe it in. Lead can build up in the body and damage the brain. Modern cars are now fitted with engines that only burn unleaded gasoline. Old cars must still use leaded gasoline. Some governments have made leaded gasoline more expensive to encourage people to get rid of their old cars. Modern cars are also fitted with a device that changes most of the poisonous gases inside an engine into less harmful ones.

Governments have made laws that punish people who allow their vehicles to pump out dirty and poisonous fumes. By making public transportation nicer and easier to use, governments encourage people to use it instead of driving—especially in large, busy cities.

What you can do

There are other ways to help reduce pollution caused by traffic. You can:
- ride a bicycle or walk
- use public transportation—a bus or a train carries a lot more people
- join or start a car pool—when people go to work, school, a club, or an event, they take turns driving.

Fact file

The amount of oil the world uses in a year would fill a lake 10 miles (16 km) long, 9 miles (14 km) wide, and 60 feet (18 m) deep.

Advantages and disadvantages of fossil fuels

Energy is at the center of our lives. It powers our world. Fossil fuels are the world's main source of energy and, every year, more and more of these non-renewable sources are used.

If we keep using fossil fuels at this rate,
- coal will run out in 250 years
- oil will run out in 90 years
- gas will run out in 60 years.

If we are to continue using fossil fuels, we need to manage them carefully and make them as clean as possible. It is better for the world to try to develop other sources of energy rather than relying on one source to meet all of its power needs.

ADVANTAGES OF FOSSIL FUELS	DISADVANTAGES OF FOSSIL FUELS
• Fossil fuels are easy and cheap to find and use.	• Burning fossil fuels is not a very efficient way to generate power. A lot of energy is wasted.
• All of our machines have been designed and built around using fossil fuels as an energy source.	• Burning releases poisonous gases, chemicals, and dirt into the air. This makes people ill and harms the environment.

Fossil fuels cause a great amount of pollution.

Fossil Fuels

Glossary

acid a type of chemical that can be harmful to people and the environment

aerosol a metal container that stores liquid under pressure and forces it out as a spray

archeologists people who study the past

artificial something made by people

barges boats that are flat bottomed

batteries containers filled with chemicals that can store or produce electricity

commercial producing something to sell

conveyor belt a moving strip that carries objects from one place to another

decay to rot or break down into something else

derrick the framework built over an oil well to raise and lower the drill

device a machine or tool designed for a particular purpose

efficient without waste

evaporate change into an invisible gas

gasoline a liquid fuel made from oil that is burned inside an engine

generator a machine that turns energy into electricity

insulated protected from heat loss

laboratory a place where scientists carry out tests

locomotives railroad engines

microbes very small living things that can only be seen under a microscope

microscope a device scientists look through, which makes very small objects look much bigger

molten rock or metal that has melted into a thick, sticky liquid

picks hand tools used for breaking rock

portable can be carried around easily

predators animals which eat other animals

refineries places where crude oil is made into gasoline and other products

remote very far away from other people

satellites spacecraft that circle the Earth and send and receive information

sea-bed the ground at the bottom of the sea

skips large metal containers for carrying coal or heavy rocks

soot a black powder that rises with the smoke when coal is burned

spherical round, like a ball

wells holes drilled into the Earth

Index

Fossil Fuels